# WHY CONFLICT MANAGEMENT DOESN'T WORK WHEN THE PROBLEM IS BULLYING

A Humanist Learning Systems Companion Book

By Jennifer Hancock

Edited by, Reginald V. Finley Sr

Published by Jennifer Hancock
Copyright 2018 by Jennifer Hancock
Published 2018

CreateSpace Edition

ISBN-13: 978-1719409148
ISBN-10: 1719409145
Authored by Jennifer Hancock
Edited by, Reginald V. Finley Sr
Published by Humanist Learning Systems

This book is also available as an e-book at most online retailers

All rights reserved. No part of this book may be used or reproduced in any manner whatsoever without written permission, except in the case of brief quotations embodied in critical articles or reviews.

This book is licensed for your personal enjoyment only.

~~~~~

# Table of Contents

CHAPTER 1: INTRODUCTION: WHY THIS BOOK?...................5

CHAPTER 2: UNDERSTANDING THE CONFLICT MODEL........7

CHAPTER 3: REDEFINING THE PROBLEM .............................9

CHAPTER 4: HIDING IN THE SHADOWS..............................13

CHAPTER 5: THE BEHAVIOR ELIMINATION MODEL............17

CHAPTER 6: THE VALUE OF REPORTING ............................25

CHAPTER 7: INVESTIGATION .............................................31

CHAPTER 8: USING A BEHAVIOR ELIMINATION MODEL.....37

CHAPTER 9: ABOUT THE AUTHOR: ...................................41

~~~~~

4

# CHAPTER 1: INTRODUCTION: WHY THIS BOOK?

In this book, we are going to discuss why conflict models don't work when the problem is bullying or harassment. You know the old saying? "If all you have is a hammer every problem looks like a nail." Well, conflict resolution only works when you are dealing with a conflict, you shouldn't use it for every interpersonal problem that arises. Different problems require different techniques to resolve.

This is the companion book to the online course Why Conflict Models Don't Work When the Problem is Bullying. In this book, we will discuss the differences between a conflict model and a bullying elimination model and how we can use elimination models to resolve both conflicts and harassment situations ethically and effectively.

Workplace bullying and harassment situations often masquerade as conflict. But they aren't. Applying a conflict resolution model to a bullying or harassment situation makes the problem worse.

Individuals and groups can benefit from this course. For more information on visit:

https://humanistlearning.com/conflictresolution/

This book contains transcripts of the course for easy home reference.

~~~~~

## CHAPTER 2: UNDERSTANDING THE CONFLICT MODEL

Don't get me wrong, <u>I love conflict resolution.</u> The problem is that conflict resolution only works if the problem is a conflict. The standard conflict resolution model is based on respect. It assumes that all parties to the problem are rational actors who will respond rationally to improved communication efforts.

The reality is that not everyone you work with is "rational" and even if they are, they may not actually want to get along with the person they are in "conflict" with. For these people, a different technique is required.

# The Thomas-Kilmann conflict model posits five ways people resolve interpersonal conflict.

<u>5 ways people deal with conflict</u>

- Accommodate
- Compromise
- Collaborate
- Compete
- Avoid
  Three of these methods constitute the advice on how to resolve conflicts and they make up what we consider to be the conflict resolution model.

Specifically, we are encouraged to accommodate, compromise and/or collaborate. But sometimes those approaches don't work and may actually make the problem worse.

The other two methods Thomas & Kilmann say people use are considered ineffective and counterproductive because they not only don't resolve the conflict; they almost always make it worse. For instance, competing is uncooperative and is essentially acknowledging the conflict is something to be won – not resolved. Avoiding the conflict doesn't resolve it either. It's uncooperative, unassertive and allows the problem to fester.

~~~~~

# CHAPTER 3: REDEFINING THE PROBLEM

To understand what technique we should use, we need to do a better job of defining exactly what our problem is. Civil disagreements and conflicts aren't really a problem. Conflicts only become an issue if they manifest as inappropriate behavior by one or more parties. Most conflict mediation approaches focus on the reasons why a person is behaving inappropriately as a way to help them communicate their needs more respectfully so that they can resolve their differences in a more behaviorally appropriate and civil manner. This works well and is a successful technique. In fact, I use this technique myself quite often.

If the problem really is an isolated incident caused by poor communication, this approach works great; but if the problem is bullying or harassment, the conflict mediation approach will not only not work, it will make things worse!

There are many reasons why a conflict mediation approach does not work with bullies and harassers:

> 1st: **bullying or harassment is almost never an isolated incident.** It is a pattern of inappropriate behavior that occurs over time.

> 2nd: **mediation allows a bully to rationalize their bad behavior.** Instead of focusing on the fact they behaved badly and should stop, you are focusing on why they behaved badly.

This does several things:

1) **It rewards them inadvertently** by giving them a platform to air their grievances as if they are legitimate, even if they aren't.

2) **It assigns equal blame** to both parties, meaning the victim of the harassment is forced to admit they may have done something to cause the harassment. This is akin to telling a robbery victim that they are responsible for the crime committed against them; or like telling a rape victim that they are responsible for making their rapist rape them! It is inappropriate and harmful to do this.

3) **It discourages reporting.** In addition to blaming the victim, you are also giving the victim negative consequences that should have gone to the bully.

4) **It makes bullying invisible.** One of the biggest problems is that the meditation model prevents you from dealing with bullying because it not only isn't optimized to handle bullying problems, bullying problems are *invisible* to the mediation model.

## Focus on What is Important

When we think of things as conflicts, they look like conflicts, even if they aren't. What we want to do instead is focus on the inappropriate behavior as being inappropriate. What some researchers call – "counterproductive workplace behavior."

The reason why an employee behaved inappropriately can only be addressed respectfully once they start behaving appropriately. When you focus on why they are behaving the way they do, they have no incentive to stop. Normal people respond well to mediation. But bullies aren't normal people. They are like little kids. If the only time you pay attention to a kid is when they act out – they will act out whenever they want your attention.

By focusing on why someone is behaving badly, you are rewarding their bad behavior. If every time they behave badly, they get to air their grievances and tell you why the other person is a horrible person, then they are being rewarded for behaving badly. It's like rewarding a child for throwing a tantrum by giving them a lollipop. What you want to do is set things up so that they are only allowed to air their grievances if they do so civilly and professionally. In other words, no ad hominem attacks! Substantive complaints only!

~~~~~

12

# CHAPTER 4: HIDING IN THE SHADOWS

Let's talk about what this looks like in practice. In the real world, it's very hard to know if you are dealing with bullying or conflict. What we know is that, if it is bullying or harassment, it will manifest as a pattern of inappropriate behavior; and that when we try to stop it, the problem will escalate.

Why behavior escalates when you remove the reward is beyond the scope of this book. If you are interested in delving into the behavioral science behind this, consider one of my other programs or books on how to stop harassment and bullying in the workplace. (https://humanistlearning.com/category/bullyingharassment/) For now, understand that the escalation of behavior is predicted to happen when the behavior is habitual and that this phenomenon even has a name – extinction burst.

Remember when I said that bullying and harassment are invisible to the conflict model? There are reasons for that, and it has to do with the frequency and consistency of reporting. Bullies like to hide in the shadows. They are only able to get away with what they do because they skirt the edge of their manager's attention. They are experts at this. When they are caught, they rationalize their behavior. The conflict resolution model enables this! As a result, managers can't see what's really happening or going on around them. They are oblivious. They can tell there is a problem, but it looks just like a conflict to them. It looks like a conflict because, if you are trained to use a conflict model to resolve the problem, then of course it looks like conflict!

## Seeing the Bigger Picture

How can we train ourselves to see the bigger picture? That takes practice and a slight tweaking of your processes. When an employee complains about another employee, instead of trying to find out why it happened (which is the conflict approach), focus on whether or not inappropriate behavior happened first.

If an employee argues that their inappropriate behavior was somehow justified, the answer is no, it wasn't. If they wanted to address this problem, they should have used the appropriate processes and behaved professionally and civilly.

The other reason why managers can't really see what is happening is because employees rarely report the bad behavior of their co-workers. There are a myriad of reasons why this is so. One of the most common ones is that when they do report bad behavior, nothing is done to stop it. In fact, what normally happens is that when they report it, things get worse. This is because of the extinction burst phenomenon, which is predicted to happen!

Our response, while well meaning, often exacerbates this. When someone behaves badly; we, instead of giving them a consequence, tend to ask them, "Why?"

Don't do that! We need to realize that, if they behaved badly, it doesn't really matter why! If they admit to what they did – give them a consequence and start monitoring them to see if they are behaving badly as a matter of habit or if it was a one-off lapse of judgement.

~~~~~

# CHAPTER 5: THE BEHAVIOR ELIMINATION MODEL

Let's talk about what a behavioral extinction or elimination model looks like and how it contrasts with a conflict mediation model.

When you take a behavioral approach, it doesn't matter why people behave badly, only that the behavior itself was inappropriate and needs to stop. When inappropriate behavior occurs, we deal with it and provide appropriate consequences. Only after the bad behavior is dealt with and the individual in question is behaving civilly again, can we begin to resolve the underlying conflict (if there is one) respectfully. Notice, this isn't in place of a conflict mediation model. It merely sets up the conditions required to use the conflict model – which is that employees behave civilly. Employees should not be allowed to bully others as a way of getting their way or forcing someone else to concede in a conflict.

## A Behavioral Approach

Let's talk about how to rein in bullying behavior using a behavioral approach.

This may seem strange but the first thing you do for someone who isn't behaving civilly is to approach them civilly: with dignity and respect. You are going to model the behavior you expect from them; and yes, this is basically the same technique you use with children.

By acknowledging the humanity of the bully, it will help us focus on training them to do and be better instead of our natural instinct which is to punish them for their bad behavior. This distinction is important because punishment is not an effective way to stop unwanted behavior. In fact, it can often make things worse, through what is known as a "vicious cycle."

There is a lot of science to back this up. A quick google scholar search for *vicious cycle punishment in humans* yields over 43,000 results - which all essentially say the same thing; and that is that punishment or negative reinforcement can become a positive reinforcement: https://scholar.google.com/scholar?hl=en&as_sdt=0%2C10&as_vis=1&q=vicious+circle+punishment+in+humans&btnG= ). In other words, negative reinforcement, is still reinforcement.

What someone behaving badly needs is for the rest of us to stop allowing them to get away with bad behavior. Collectively we need to stop rewarding them when they bully. The victims, bystanders, and bosses need to stop rewarding them. They should be rewarded and praised only when they put their talents and basic nature (which may be aggressive) to good use, not when they are dominating their fellow employees inappropriately. In other words, we need to stop playing the same game the bully is playing and stop complying with their demands when they demand things in an inappropriate way.

## Consequences

Bullies need consequences. Don't confuse consequences with punishment, and don't use consequences as punishment. Punishment not only doesn't work – it will probably makes things worse.

The consequences that work best to stop an unwanted behavior is nothing - a neutral response. The bully doesn't get what they want. That's it! If what they wanted was social status – deny them that. If what they wanted was to get their way – deny them that.

The victim denies a bully their reward by responding calmly and reporting them for inappropriate behavior. Their manager notes their inappropriate behavior and calmly redirects them to more appropriate behavior and reminds them what the company policy is and that the expectation is that they will behave civilly and professionally and then files the report. In other words, you put them on notice.

When the bully starts to argue about what the other person did to make them behave poorly, they are redirected to the proper civil way to deal with these "conflicts." If the other person was behaving badly – which they will probably claim – then they should report them. What should not happen is that the manager does not respond or allow the bully to air the complaints of the bully until or unless the bully uses the proper methods to bring up problems in a civil way.

Again, this isn't done to punish them. It's about retraining them. It is only to make it clear that not only are they not going to get their way when they behave badly, but that every time they behave badly it is noted in their record. If they prove incapable of behaving civilly they will end up losing their job. This isn't emotional. It isn't punishment. It's a natural consequence for people who behave badly if your company has a policy to not tolerate bad behavior.

Obviously, responding to bullying behavior neutrally and documenting their inappropriate behavior isn't enough. If you are dealing with bullying or harassment and not just a conflict, then when the bully stops getting their way and they lose their reward, it will trigger an extinction burst.

## Extinction Bursts

An extinction burst is an escalation of behavior that occurs when a reward is removed. This is predicted behavior IF the problem is ongoing harassment or bullying. If you are dealing with bullying, this means the bully will get more aggressive and retaliate when they lose their reward. If the problem is a conflict manifesting as bad behavior, redirection to appropriate behavior should be enough to resolve the problem.

If you trigger an extinction burst by insisting they behave civilly, that pretty much tells you this is a bullying situation and not a normal conflict. People who are NOT in the habit of behaving badly – will take your advice and follow your directions on how to resolve the problem. People who are in the habit of behaving badly – will behave more badly.

Again – this is predicted behavior – use this knowledge to your advantage to tell the difference between conflict and harassment and who is really at fault.

## Looking for a Pattern of Behavior

Remember what I said about the conflict model? Once a conflict is resolved, it's considered done. In a behavior elimination model, we are expecting a possible escalation of bad behavior. We are actively looking to see if this is a pattern that plays out over time.

If the problem is resolved and the behavior doesn't escalate, great. But if it does escalate, we are ready for it. And by ready, I mean that we are going to document and respond promptly to the escalation of behavior to interrupt it. This has to be done promptly and consistently to work.

If you really do have a problem employee, document their pattern of behavior. If they escalate, blow out, and/or have their extinction burst, your documentation will help you make a compelling case if you end up having to terminate them. It will also help you defend yourself if the victim sues as this same documentation will indicate what actions were taken to stop the harassment. Plus, every time a bully is caught and their behavior is documented as inappropriate, they not only are not getting their reward, their bad behavior is jeopardizing their job.

How bad can an extinction burst or escalation get? Extinction bursts are also known as blow outs, and they can and do get really really messy! Essentially, when someone who is used to harassing and bullying suddenly can't get away with it anymore, their behavior escalates and becomes so egregious that no one can ignore it anymore. The good news is that nowadays – they leave documentation trails in the form of emails so you can terminate them if it becomes necessary.

Just a word of caution: If the behavior is already physically violent and includes threats – you need to take into account what an escalation of behavior will look like and take serious safety precautions before you trigger an extinction burst. Because violence – escalates to even more violence!

# Recap of Behavioral Extinction Process

- Respect/Dignity
- Non-Compliance
- Consequences
- Costs

# The Importance of Being Consistent

The escalation or extinction burst is a bully raising the cost of defying them by being more aggressive. They are trying to eliminate the costs and consequences and get their rewards back by doing what they've always done – behave badly. If behaving badly stops working – they tend to behave more badly. Again – it's predicted they will do this.

Your compassion may call on you as the manager to have mercy on them but actually, by giving in and giving them a break you make it harder on them to transition to the better behavior that you want. The reason for this is that every act of leniency creates a variable reinforcement schedule. Variable reinforcement is known to strengthen behaviors. The most compassionate thing you can do for a bully is to be 100% consistent with them when they behave badly. Follow your policies regarding civil behavior. Every time. Consistency is what gets the behavior to stop.

This is so important, I'm going to repeat it. Leniency will draw out the problem and make it harder to solve. Consistency will help you stop the problem behavior quicker.

~~~~~

## CHAPTER 6: THE VALUE OF REPORTING

Our goal is to not let bullies get away with inappropriate behavior while simultaneously encouraging them towards more civil behavior. To do this we need to consistently respond to bad behavior and encourage and reward good behavior. We can't do that unless people report bad behavior. So we need to reconsider how we think of and deal with reports of this nature.

Most of the time, reporting processes are put in place and then management discourages reporting so the reporting process isn't used. No one is reporting a problem, so we must not have a problem. Right? Uh, wrong.

According to statistics from the Workplace Bullying Institute, 30 to 40% of all workers are bullied. 10% are being bullied chronically. (http://www.workplacebullying.org/wbiresearch/wbistudies/) This is a problem whether it is recognized as one or not. If you want a better work environment for everyone, you need to document problems and have a reporting process that supports the behavior extinction process.

## We need to encourage reporting.

If someone behaves poorly, you need to know about it. You can't help an employee being victimized if you don't know it is happening. The other reason to encourage reporting is because if the problem is harassment or bullying, it is a pattern of behavior and you need ongoing reporting to document that pattern and you can only do that if people report it. In order to get your employees to report problems you need to encourage them and reward them for reporting things to you. Why? Because most people understand that reporting things without support makes things worse. They may not understand the science of extinction bursts, but they do understand the concept of retaliation.

In order to get people to report, they need encouragement, but more importantly, they need to see progress being made. If you handle reports of harassment poorly, people won't use your reporting system as it's not in their best interest to do so.

If on the other hand, you handle it well and fairly, and people can see that the documentation is being used to build a case against a person for possible termination - people will start reporting and you will find they are actually eager to report. They have just been waiting for someone to take them seriously!

In order to encourage reporting you have to make your system easy to use. If it isn't easy, your employees won't report. There are systems that can be integrated into your computer network cheaply. There are apps that allow reporting in the moment, complete with photos. This can be done easily and there are out-of-the-box systems you can purchase that will allow people to report what is happening using the tools they already have at their disposal.

If you are worried about false reporting or overreporting – don't be. Most companies have an under-reporting problem, not an over reporting problem. Even if someone decides to use the reporting process to harass someone else, which can and does happen, your investigation process will help you sort that out and identify who is the real problem.

Don't assume that because someone is making a ton of reports, they are making false reports. Harassment most often manifests as a bunch of small incidences that don't seem that important in isolation, but when taken as a pattern of behavior, makes sense. You need all of that reporting to document the pattern of behavior.

*FOR EXAMPLE:*
Let's imagine an employee is being harassed. Every day they get snide remarks, their lunch is stolen, they are put down. Jokes are told about them while they are present, and much more. They report that they are being harassed.

The manager asks them to give an example. So they do. They say, while I was in this meeting, this other person said something derogatory. The manager then goes to the accused and asks them, did you say this? Most likely, the accused is going to say no. Of course not. Or, yes, but it was a joke. The manager tells the accused to be more understanding and to not joke as much. As far as the manager is concerned, the problem is solved. But it isn't. All that happened was that the victim made an attempt to get help and the manager attempted to help them, but the bully was able to rationalize their behavior and get off without any real consequence.

Now let's imagine that this same victim reports being harassed and the manager asks them, not for an example, but for them to document what is happening – to report everything that happens. A documentation log is given to the alleged victim and they dutifully fill it out. The manager looks at it and sees 30 reports of what appears to be really minor things. Jokes told, looks made, workloads not distributed equally, someone "forgot" to invite them to a meeting, etc.

The average manager looking at this sort of documentation is going to wonder whether the person reporting is just really super sensitive and over-reacting. They may even be annoyed that they have to deal with this because, this isn't just a quick - have a talk and resolve it sort of problem. What is being alleged is messy and ongoing. There is a natural resistance to dealing with this sort of problem.

But, they take the report and confront the alleged bully about the alleged pattern of behavior. The alleged bully looks at it and is stunned, and floats the idea that - yes, indeed, they are having problems with the alleged victim and that the victim is a problem for whatever reason. The alleged bully, will play on the inclinations of the manager to not want to deal with this and give them an excuse to not deal with it by painting the alleged victim as being the problem. This is called - gaslighting.

The alleged victim, instead of getting help, is now viewed as the problem. They did what they were asked to do which is to report everything. But all they succeeded in doing - was annoy their manager and make themselves look bad.

These sorts of reporting scenarios play out in offices around the world. They are the reason why victims of harassment are hesitant to report what is happening. The way to change this is to reward reporting. And that means understanding that when you ask people to report everything, the report is going to include a LOT of little things that on their own, are insignificant, but taken together as a pattern of behavior, constitute harassment.

Do not view what seems like an excessive log of "microaggressions" as evidence of false reporting. That is exactly how harassment in the workplace tends to manifest.

~~~~~

## CHAPTER 7: INVESTIGATION

Let's assume you have a way for employees to report problems, and that your employees have started using the system. Now what? Well, now you have to look into the allegations being made. This is easier than it seems. Either the inappropriate behavior occurred or it didn't. Period. Remember, this is bullying/harassment reporting and response, not mediation reporting and response.

The investigation should be as prompt as possible while still being fair. Here's why. Delays in dealing with a bully makes things worse. It creates a variable response that strengthens the behavior you don't want. Additionally, if it is harassment or bullying, there will be additional bullying and retaliation that will occur before you finish your investigation. You have to warn the person reporting bullying that this may happen and let them know exactly what you want them to do when (not if) it happens. Let them know that if this person retaliates, this is what you want them to do.

We need to be fair in an investigation, even if it will take time, but there should be no delay in notifying the manager and the accused that a report has been made and an investigation is going to happen.

Given technology available, this is totally doable and putting the accused on notice that there is possibly going to be a consequence will have the same effect as an actual consequence. If they are in the habit of harassing people – they will retaliate. And if they do, you will know you are dealing with a problem employee.

If you have set up your investigation properly to look for escalating behavior and retaliation – you will be able to document that as it occurs.

You should have at least one person ultimately responsible for overseeing the investigation process. That person will assign someone to be responsible for investigating the claim. This person will provide follow ups and due dates for the investigation to be completed. What they need to know is who, what, where, when, plus documentation. Who did it? Who was the victim? Who is the accused bully? They need to know, what exactly happened. State specifics, not general terms. Where did it happen? When did it happen? Who witnessed it? And whether there is any supporting documentation or evidence to back up the allegation. This will give the person responsible for investigating the report what they need to investigate quickly. Ideally, the very same day.

The sooner these things are resolved, the better. Consistency is key. Delays cause variable reinforcement and that makes things worse. A lot worse.

## Resolve Quickly but Fairly

You have to be fair – but you can still notify all parties that a report has been made and is being investigated. This is important because delays in response, cause the problem to continue and get worse.

*FOR EXAMPLE:*
My son rides the bus to school. When he was in third grade, he got punched in the stomach by a kindergartner. He was walking down the aisle of the bus and this little kid just punched him in the stomach. My son reported this to the driver, who told him to sit down.

When he got home, he told me what happened. I called the principal of the school to let her know. I also called the bus department to alert them as well. I knew from previous experience that it can take a few days for a report of an incident on the bus to make its way to the principal and I know those delays can put more kids at risk.

The next morning, the bus driver thanked me for making those calls. She told me that particular kid punched several kids before and that she had written him up eight times. This kid was two incident reports away from being suspended from riding the bus, and the principal didn't even know it was happening!!!! The parent of this kid, didn't even know it was happening!!!! All because the process was slow.

Let me put this a different way: eight kids were hurt because a behavior problem was allowed to fester because the reporting process to handle this sort of behavior problem was so slow from the kid's perspective, it might as well have been non-existent.

The problem wasn't a lack of concern. The bus driver was concerned and taking action. The principal was concerned and taking action. And, the parent was concerned and as soon as she found out, made her son stop. The problem was the process was too slow and the child was able to continue their bad behavior without immediate consequence. The problem was that the child was not notified, that they were being written up and that their parent would find out. As far as this kid was concerned, he was getting away with it. He wasn't, but he thought he was because no one told him otherwise.

Simple tweaks to this system could have eliminated the problem almost immediately. First, if the bus driver had told the child to: a) not to do it again, and b) that they were being written up and that their parents were being notified, that might have nipped this problem in the bud. Instead, the driver told the reporting kids to sit down and didn't write up the report until that evening. If they had given the kid a slip to give to their parent that evening the first time it happened, things might have been different.

My point is: even if you have to investigate and that might take time, you can still put the alleged offender on notice that specific behavior was noticed and being included in a report. This will allow the investigation to take its course, while still providing near immediate feedback to the parties involved which is essential to getting the behavior to stop.

## Bullying reporting and response.

Even though you are looking at behavior in context of a larger pattern, you are still dealing with a single incidence of inappropriate behavior. These single incidences are fairly easy to verify, disprove or mark uncertain (which means you can't prove or disprove it).

Either someone said something or posted something they shouldn't have, or they didn't. Either there were witnesses who can back it up or there aren't. The big difference is because you are dealing with things in near to real time you aren't allowing things to drag on and escalate or for evidence to disappear. It's actually easier to see, identify and respond to these things when you don't let it drag out. You handle the problems when they are still molehills instead of waiting for them to develop into mountains.

One way to speed up the process is to understand that the goal of an investigation is to determine whether an incident happened or not. This is fairly easy to do quickly.

Determining whether the behavior was inappropriate or not may take longer. What to do about it may take longer still. Those are decisions made AFTER you have verified that yes – the incident in question really did happen. The *did it happen* investigation needs to be quick and the results verified quickly. The – *why did it happen* and *was it really inappropriate or not* part of the investigation can take more time.

By verifying incidences quickly – not passing judgement on them, but just verifying they occurred and the communication of the results make it very clear very quickly that bullies aren't going to be able to get away with it and this discourages bullying behavior as everyone becomes accustomed to the new norm and expectations. It also gives notice to false reporters that they are being caught. The quicker the response, the quicker the new more appropriate behavior patterns are learned and the quicker the bad behavior is extinguished and that's good for everyone! The prompt response also creates confidence that the reports are being taken seriously.

Most times, reports are made and even if they are being worked on, it's like reporting to a black hole. You make the report and nothing happens for a month or two and eventually you hear about it again. That sort of delay discourages further reporting and enables bullies because they are able to continue bullying and retaliate while the investigation is taking place, usually, without consequence. The delay also makes the response variable instead of consistent. And when it comes to bullies, variable responses make things worse! Consistent responses get the behavior to stop.

Finally, you need to make sure that staff is trained on what to do if the accused retaliates, which is to report every additional incidence of retaliation or bad behavior. Because this is bullying reporting, you are expecting the accused to retaliate. Everyone should be prepared for this and know what to do when retaliation occurs. This again, inspires confidence in the staff and discourages further bullying. Plus, reporting of any and all retaliation attempts allows you to see the full pattern of what transpires, including the escalation of the unwanted behavior. You will need this documentation if you decide to terminate the employee.

~~~~~

## CHAPTER 8: USING A BEHAVIOR ELIMINATION MODEL

Once the investigation is done, a decision has to be made on what to do about it.

First, both the victim, the bully, the reporting party and the manager should be notified of the findings. (validated, false, or uncertain) It's a good idea to have some standard consequences if people are found to be behaving poorly. For instance, denigrating comments would be handled one way. Threats another. Actual violence yet another. Remedial training might be required.

Assistance and further training for the victim is always appreciated and helpful and will help the victim continue to report what is happening to them which is essential to continuing the extinction process and to the building of a case file if it turns out that termination is necessary.

A system for more closely monitoring the bully (assuming they are found to be guilty) needs to be put into place to help monitor them through the extinction process to ensure that the behavioral extinction is completed.

Steps should be taken to protect the victim from further violence and harassment. If the bully and victim need to be separated, it is the bully that should be isolated to protect the rest of the employees. Do not ever isolate the victim to protect them. This will just make their situation worse and reward the bully. Most bullying is an attempt to socially isolate the victim. Don't do that for the bully. Isolate the bully instead. Always remember. If one person is being victimized, others are as well, they just may not have had the courage to report it.

If you do find out that one of your employees is bullying, assume they have multiple victims because they most likely do. The person behaving badly is the one who needs to be isolated and their ability to function without supervision limited. The other thing restricting the bully with increased supervision will do is serve to act as a negative consequence which will raise the cost of behaving poorly.

The purpose of this is not to punish the bully, but simply a recognition that they are undergoing retraining and need to be monitored through the process so that the behavioral extinction happens as quickly as possible. As always, this needs to be consistent and applied to everyone equally. If not, loop holes and special exceptions will be exploited by bullies and you will never eliminate the problem.

Remember, consistency is what eliminates the behavior. Leniency makes things worse. Don't fall into that trap. Bullies cost more than they provide and you are better off eliminating the behavior or them if necessary than tolerating them for expediency. The cultural shift that this sort of reporting and response creates will astonish you.

### *FINAL THOUGHTS*
A behavioral approach is not mutually exclusive with the conflict mediation approach. They work together wonderfully. When you insist that your employees

behave professionally, you are prioritizing and rewarding respectful behavior. When employees treat each other with respect, civilized conflict resolution takes care of itself.

~~~~~

# CHAPTER 9: ABOUT THE AUTHOR:

Jennifer Hancock is a mom, author of several books, and founder of Humanist Learning Systems. Jennifer is unique in that she was raised as a freethinker and is considered one of the top speakers and writers in the world of Humanism today. Her professional background is varied including stints in both the for profit and non-profit sectors. She has served as Director of Volunteer Services for the Los Angeles SPCA, sold international franchise licenses for a biotech firm, was the Manager of Acquisition Group Information for a ½ billion-dollar company and served as the executive director for the Humanists of Florida. When she became a mother, she decided to stay at home, but that didn't last long. Shortly after her son was born, she published her first book, The Humanist Approach to Happiness: Practical Wisdom. Her speaking and teaching business coalesced into the founding of Humanist Learning Systems which provides online personal and professional development training in humanistic business management and science-based harassment training that actually works.

# More Learning from Jennifer Hancock

*OTHER BOOKS BY JENNIFER HANCOCK*
- The Humanist Approach to Happiness
- Jen Hancock's Handy Humanism Handbook
- The Bully Vaccine
- The Humanist Approach to Grief and Grieving
- How to Win Arguments Without Arguing
- Ending Harassment & Retaliation in the Workplace
- Why Bullies Bully & How to Stop Them Using Science
- Reality Based Decision Making for Effective Strategy Development
- How to De-Escalate Conflicts Using Behavioral Science

*COURSES TAUGHT BY JENNIFER HANCOCK*
- Workplace Bullying for HR professionals
- Living Made Simpler
- An Introduction to Humanism
- Socratic Jujitsu: How to Win Arguments Without Argument
- Why Conflict Resolution Doesn't Work When the Problem is Bullying
- Bridging the Generational Divide: Millennials vs. Boomers
- Ending Harassment and Retaliation in the Workplace
- Reality Based Decision Making for Effective Strategy Development

- How to De-escalate Conflicts Using Behavioral Science
- Why is Change so Hard?
- Principles of Humanistic Management
- 7 Sins of Staff Management
- How to Handle Cranky Customer Problems
- New Manager Orientation
- Humanist Group Leadership Lessons
- Sexual harassment training that works – general
- Sexual harassment training that works – AB 1825
- Stop Bullying in our Workplace – Staff Training
- Sexual Harassment Compliance Training
- No Fear Act training
- Planning for Personal Success!
- Talking to your child about death
- The Bully Vaccine Toolkit
- How to talk to your child's school about bullying
- Why Bullies Bully & How to Stop Them

*CONNECT WITH ME ONLINE:*
- Twitter: http://twitter.com/#!/JentheHumanist
- Facebook: http://www.facebook.com/JentheHumanist
- Or sign up for my mailing list: http://eepurl.com/c3LuI

The End

#####

44

www.ingramcontent.com/pod-product-compliance
Lightning Source LLC
Chambersburg PA
CBHW030038230526
45472CB00002B/566